Threads

By Karin Jervert

The Knots We Tie

For Honey

On a late winter night,
I gather up inside,
Checking on all the ones I love.

Are they accounted for tonight?

And we tuck away the future days,
Because everyone is here on this night —
Everyone beloved is safe.

We must know who is beloved,
To know who is missing come spring —
To know just what can be lost in a season.

With all the messengers of my mind,
I reach out with silent prayers,
Waiting for some returning sound —

* * *

A whisper, a heartbeat, a feeling.

And I am reassured and relieved,
 These knots I've tied —
Unbroken.

Even if I know,
Even if I know,
The winds will change.

Deep in the December of a death no one can
negotiate.
Not me,
Not by the power of Love even.
Not by all the gifts of the Gods —

Nothing will keep these kinds of knots tied forever.

Tonight, I hold the rolls,
Filled with all of your names,
Along with the lost and the left behind —
Thanking time again,
It has not come for any more of my beloved
friends,
On this night.

And I surrender to sleep,

Feeling as if I am one of these beloveds,
Not just the one who tied the knot,
Of a golden thread —

But a fiber of it, too.

To the poets and the artists,
The mad and the mourning.
To all the weavers, the seers and the
dreamers

Seed Poem

The artist always remembers,
There are no mistakes in this universe —
There are no mistakes at all.

Every failure a seed poem,
Seed poem.

What tree will grow from such confused desire?
What threads will tie a knot,
What fates will be bound?

The veil re-tells the story of you,
To all the souls listening on the other side.

My breathing has become filled with 100s of
generations of hope,
And the air feels so different now.

I listen for changes and I never choose a pattern.
Never hold one fault line with more honor than
another,
One frame,

One timeline,
They are all the same.

None more sacred.

Never choose —
Because the human mind only mirrors,
The consciousness of all creatures.

So, what net will you build?
Each crossroads a crystal.
As many possibilities,
As there are dimensions.

****

So much depends on the first line of a poem —
Written on a slip of paper on a dormitory floor.
Blown away one day,
When she came barging in.

Loud and rude and full of assumptions,
Like she owned every inch of my life —
And, honestly, maybe she did already.

My Beatrice,
My Sophia.

Barging in just to tell me there was kindness left

here still,
Then to slip out the opposite way,
Just like everyone else ever since —

Quietly.

An awkward letting go,
A sideways glance,
Without goodbye.

The first line,
Simple.

My Sophia on the floor of a dormitory,
Blown away one day,

"The word made flesh."
It said.

Then nothing made sense.
And I listen for any changes for 20 years on.

Some sounds of death come at the beginning.
Some sounds of hope come at the end.
Some sounds of fear come in the middle,
When courage fails then is born again.

You do not love the Artist the way I have,
And not know exactly what has been going on —

Seed poem.
Seed poem.

I see you growing.

Red Threads

She is Free to Go

She is free to go,
The spirit, the soul of hope.
The girl I used to be.

Let her skin be shed like the snake's.
Let the gift of friendship be honored then.

Let her spirit be released.

Release all the ways I look at life sideways,
All the ways anonymity haunts me.
All the days I spend alone.
With all the windows open.

I invite her to feel how the air travels on her skin,
As the old ways leave with the wind.

She says, let this be the broken curse of the
maiden.

Let us finally see.

It's going to be alright.
The way we grieve and scream,
Yet feel so quiet with one another.

The way we forget who we are.

The snake takes what it has offered.
His precious gift of stealth and stealing.
Let the burden leave with him.
And may he not have to bare it either.

Let it be taken to heaven,
Where the prayers of the maiden are heard,
Where they are loud and clear like bells.

And let Bobby meet the death of her at the gates,
Where prayers become sounds and songs.

Where boys become gods and girls saviors,
teachers, and sages

Let my longing leave me now,
Let it leave on the back of a snake.
Out with the wind through all these open
windows.

Let this be enough.

Red

The color Red is harmony —
Contrast and cooperation.

The sound of it next to the sirens,
Makes me feel like crying.

The sound of the color Red,
Next to life creates a kind of music within —
Counterpoint.

Somewhere,
I'm hearing the story of creation —
It's sweet, ugly urgency.

And the slowing down of time.
So it can be savored like the only thing there is to
eat,
At the edge of death.

Praying Out Loud

*A friend said to me one day
that the most frightening thing
these days is to pray out loud.*

Here,
A great shame has been made of my soul.

The seer.
The priestess.
The bard, the jester.
The stag.
The game.

My neck under the boot of this rage —
I am somedays dumb and cannot speak.

I used to be proud of how I survived.
Waiting — impatiently — for the world to stop
battering me,
Like a child might wait for a treat.

Now, after all these years,

I just ask why —

Why survive?

I am an abomination of darkness in your mind.
I should leave you with a less painful fate,
Like joy and love and everlasting life.

I'm a poet after all —
Shouldn't I deliver something other than death?
Something other than the song of a rage filled
priestess?

No, I am of the Goddess
I deliver the truth of pain,
And no other reason to survive than devotion.

Yet, I can't speak much to devotion,
Such a failed priestess I am.
Always reluctant to prostrate to things unseen.
Eternally suspicious of gravity,
And the fact of things.

Why praise a Goddess aloud,
When she is ravaged by the sound?
In a world that is cross crossed with the poisoned
blood of her priestesses,
Are there any true devotions now?

Or is there just Her rage to wash it all away?
The wrath of a forgotten way?
I wish you all good luck and grace in that
exchange.

Maybe you could find an offering,
That fits into the hand of a new born baby,
One that becomes a memory of the ancient ways.

****

My girlhood was lost,
And the woman I could have been buried deep in
the Earth,
While her soul weeps with the stars in the night
sky —
Writing poetry.

I wish for only one word to be heard,
And not just by the mountains —
A word planted like a seed.

****

Why adorn a maiden now?

I drown, day in and day out —
Shedding these offerings onto the ground.
A seed, an unknown flower.

None the less,
Here,
Here it is —
A prayer.

****

Can I still see the high priestess in me?
No —
I see a girl who cannot grow.
A girl unbecoming.
Remembering that night she stared into the River.
Hardly 15 —
Eating songs that she did not sing,
Food she did not grow.
Trying to move her body like everyone else,
Because it seemed to ease all the ways her life felt
like hell.

All the ways she lived in a void of the nothings she
could not tell.

****

One night at 42 she dreamt she was adorned,
By Water and the West.
A necklace clasped around her neck.
A woman,

Someone she thought she might have known once,
Said she would see it done.

* * *

But I woke up alone.
Remembering all the adornments that had already
come.
The dreams that roamed lost in years of violence.
And how they happened every day until it wasn't
clear,
Why they chose me any longer —
So steeped in silence I was.

****

What strange thing did I seek?
What strange thing had I lost?

Why did it matter if it was in my hands or anyone
else's —
The Goddess' kiss?

The true question is:
In what world is she barren?
In what world is she alone?

Adorned or not,
The maiden's robe is red and tattered from time
travel.
Lined with the yellow of the strained brow of my

mother.
Of the mother I never was —
The mother I couldn't be.
The mother who turned and ran in the fields that
day.

The mother who sacrificed it all for a mustard seed.

****

What does an adornment serve these days,
But to wake the rage of a starved Goddess?
To open her eyes to the betrayal of those who let
the moon set on their devotion?
Hypnotized by the promise of a lie.

To put her pale blue hand into the worn out minds
Of those who can do nothing but hope life is more
than having once loved her,
Once known her truth.
Her terrible truth.

****

It's so simple to my heart.
But all I've been is a question again and again,
To those with answers of their own,
Who will not listen.

So, I hold her terrifying blue hand and let her
whisper to me,
Just so she might live again.
Singing her alive in your mind.

Why adorn a maiden then?

Why raise her word?

Why listen to the divine?

When it will be divided,
And divided again,
With each atrocity —
Each fracturing self,
Embodied in yet another poet?

****

I tell you,
You best feed Her something other than poison for
the favor.
So many have suffered,
Burnt in the flames of remembering.

And I know love always writes the major hymns,
I know this rage is a phase of the moon.
But what is truly of love here?
I cannot find it.

No horse will lead me there.
Perhaps because I have nothing left to bleed for it.

* * *

What a lost tome that could be.

How I want my one word,
To be a word of hope and not one of rage and
warning.
How I breathe in and out all day long wanting it.

The Girls I Used To Be

My life holds the history of all the girls I used to
be.

And I've been trying to heal them all.
But, I don't know what that means really —
To make art for anything beyond beauty,
Anything beyond resonance.

To make art only for ugly little me,
Me who has no more wishes to be pretty,
Or to make beautiful, pleasing things,
And doesn't need your fucking sympathy.

I have always created with fire.
I have always create with pain.
Lessons learned in lack,
Lessons learned from being locked away.

Though my story may seem flimsy,
I know when a woman is lying,
I know what's being withheld in the end.

The walls helped me see.
The walls helped me see.

Yes,
The walls helped me see,
All the inequity baked into this half cocked reality,
And I am fucking angry.
Tired of the lies and secrecy.

And I know the searing pain of putting a cigarette
out on my arm,
Again and again at 17,
Asking why all the time, screaming.

She knows each and every lie she told.

And she knows,
I want to be sacred.

She doesn't want me to be
Because of how things always seemed so unworthy
of those bloody poems.
So sacred they were,
She's been bloodied before.

And the walls made her see.
And the walls made her see.

* * *

The walls made her see all the ways you never
really loved me.

All the ways pain was the only thing that paid the
bills.

And she hated the smell of my body.
She hated how tired I was all the fucking time.
She would call me stupid, too,
But even she knows now where that all goes to —

More searing nights,
And blood red eyes,
Not even she can handle anymore.

For Kate

For Kate.
The woman.
The threat.

For Kate.
The woman.
The threat.

For Kate the one who heard the song,
Let it fill all the space inside her,
Then looked around —

Everything turned up empty.
So, she got angry.

The one who's vengeance for all the ways we harm
each other,
Is Love.
Is Love.

When it can be.

                              * * *

For Kate.
The woman.
The threat.

The girl who's mind was locked away.
Locked away,
Again and again.
Where she still bangs and bangs,
On walls made 6 feet thick of cinderblock,
Or crumbling college dorm plaster,
Or the easily cleaned,
Tiny green tiles in a solitary cell.

So easy to wash away the pain.

For Kate.
The Woman.
The threat.

The girl who bangs and bangs,
And bleeds on those walls.

For Kate.
The woman.
The threat.

For all the girls who bleed,
Don't forget them.

* * *

They bleed for us.

And Me, A Failure

I wake each day as if I had sinned in my sleep.
So familiar is the disappointment of my flesh,
And consciousness.

Once we made offerings to the Moon and the Sun.
Then to the many Gods.
Then to the One.

Now to Man.
Then for sin.

Never to each other,
Now to none.

And nothing is good again.

My body not saved,
My body not saved.

Call Me Crazy

Yes, they will call me crazy.
All day and all night they will pray,
they are not as crazy as me.

And I will sit in dusk's light,
Moved.
Moved by the music.
 Writing poetry,

Free to be moved.

Being different.
Dirty.
Diseased.

Human.

And I tell myself that one day I might bleed for it,
Die for for being me.

I might bleed for being that thing that crumbles

the walls,
And reveals the in-between.
Between,
You and I.

For being that thing that starts the prayers rolling
off tongues,
Overjoyed.
Singing,
"I'm crazy.
I'm crazy.
And so are you!

Mad, too.
Mad, too!"

The Joke

The maze of self,
A circle of obscurations —

Preferences.
Avoidances.
Denials and deaths.

I'm dreaming,

When my breath should be bringing alive the real inside me,
But it only brings jealousy.

Asking me,
"What gift am I to be given?
For this suffering I've endured?"

The joke of course is always more.

But maybe grace might come.

* * *

Sometimes she appears and I see her there.
Waiting in some poem.

27

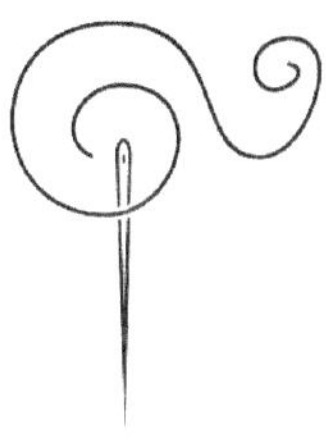

Blue Threads

We Are Warriors

Walking in this nightmare with a small soul in toe,
My shadow,
Down a dark hallway.

A door rumbling and roaring.
The house around us,
Falling down because of the wind of the sound.

You say to me full of honorable suspicion,
Citing all those years I left you alone in this
memory,

"Are you here to protect me?"

Just the way I see your hands reach for me,
I know the answer,
Now,
Will always be,

"Yes."

* * *

No matter how the storm gathers and the winds
blow,
How the house shakes.
How the man inside grunts and roars.
How the doors are darkened.

"I am here."
I say.

I am here to reframe the pain.
To walk that hallway.
And to take the blame when you should not have
had to.

To help you speak your truth when you are told to
keep silent.

And to honor you for keeping so many promises.
Gathered together for so long in such tiny hands.

"I am here."
I say.

To sing to you so you can hear the way love is
always louder.
How sometimes the sound of it can float above the

hurts and the tears.

"I am here."
I say.

No matter how my own hands shake,
Facing the storm.
The roar.
The door.

No matter how my heart shatters watching your
face,
Watching me,
Walking in this nightmare —
With all our fears.

I will be our shield.

I am not afraid to see what's behind the veil

You ask me,
"How are you not afraid to open that door, it's
screaming so loud…"
"Because you need to show me what's in there." I
say.

We deserve to know,

Whatever we see.
And I am here to witness it,
Even if you were alone that day.
Even if I can't help by try to close the door, too.

The winds will always open it again.

I'm old enough now to know how we choose,
To spare the ones we love from the things we
ourselves cannot bare.

"I love you," I say.
"It was never a secret to keep forever.
These kinds of broken promises are sacred."

Our bravery unmatched,
We can walk through any door,
Hear any roar,
Face any storm.

We are warriors.

A Prayer at the Gate

I am a soldier drunk on Berry juice.
Trying to save myself from the horrors of war,
With just the sound of my voice.

I stomp my feet and I scream.
While the beat of the drum in my ears,
Pumps blood to my limbs,
And through my heartbreaker's heart.

The bomb always overhead.

I am a soldier dreaming of a better way.
Swinging my words in the forest,
Suffering metaphor,
Rages and riddles.

And I am weary.

Sometimes the path is gone from me,
And I am only trying to save what's left.

*　*　*

I've been wounded in the war of everyone else's
angels.
The songs they sing —
Rhythms of hate,
Of Red and the end of things.

I am a poet,
Drunk on the muses drink.

I am a heart that bleeds for peace.
For lifetimes and lifetimes and lifetimes,
I speak for my angel.
While you unfurl what is real,
And show me all these pointless horrors.

Here I am at your gates,
Feeling full of rage more than grief,
To tell the truth,

With your blood on my words,
Searching the sky for my regrets.

I Cannot Hold Up This Sky

I cannot hold up this sky.

Each and every time,
It crumbles,
And falls like crystal rain.

Millions of mirrors,
Reflecting everything.

Everything I wished I could have been.

I am here again.
And, I am not enough again.

And yet, here I am again,
I offer it up again.

I chose a long time ago,
Not to follow.
I chose a long time ago,

The sacrificial fire —
Knowing it was my own spark that fed the flames.

Don't tell me again,
If it's your sky or mine,
That I'm so crushed by.

I turn to you and ask,
"Did you make this?"

These millions of mirrors,
Rain drops of all these hopes and fears.
This ocean of sky at our feet —
Reflecting everything.

I chose a long time ago,
That no matter what,
I was enough.

And I will offer it up.
So, here I am again trying to hold it up.

Ode to Love & Violence

To all the ways we fail to love,
To all the ways we use violence,
With no idea at all what we have done.

Father to son — friends, strangers…everyone.

To all my wounds,
And to all my weapons.

To all those who swung the blade.

To all the ways we drive each other mad,
To all the games we play.

Mothers, daughters - friends, strangers…everyone.

The the endless parade of the dead.

Here's to it just being how things are done. —
Between those we love.

* * *

A dance to the death.
Each wound a kiss —
A sending off into the abyss.

To how we love each other,
So imperfect —
To the violence of it.

The Violence of Other Men

My father covets the violence of other men,
Men who know how to control women.
Who know how to make the whole world submit
to them.

I asked him once,
"Why would you long for such a thing?"
And he doesn't know,
But I do.

I do.

Because he is a boy who couldn't stop the pain.
A boy left on the church steps.
Wrenched from his heritage.

His father, a mad man who played the fool,
And never came home again.
His mother with little to remember of herself.

* * *

My father covets the violence of other men.
He wishes he could have been strong enough,
To make her stay.
To force her to love him enough —
To be true.

What a knot of blame and helplessness —
How I feel caught in his eyes most days.
A lesson in his text book:

How to control a woman.

How to control anyone.
How to control a world,
The universe, his fate, my fate,

How to control love.

When a boy just needed to be held.

To be kept.
Kept safe.
Kept warm.
Kept.
Kept like a worthy boy.
Like a good boy was.

* * *

Like all the boys that mattered were.

Sometimes I can't keep up with all the poems I
need to write about my father.

How to beat a world,
How to beat a woman.

Look at how well the others do it.

I wish I were him.
I wish I knew how to use my violence —
To be kept,
Not to be forgotten,
Not to be thrown away,
To keep me from the darkness of my days —

How do I make people stay?
If only I knew the words to say.

Am I Free of You?

Deep in the weeds of my more precious faces and
feelings,
I choke out my intention,
To find the sound of blue again.

The sound of stones and the Ocean.

Despite what I'd like to tell you,
I've always wanted to be a rock star —
Since I was 5.

But, then again,
I am always wondering,
Am I free the web of it,
Laid so carefully,
Creatively?

Spirit test.
Lyric nest.

* * *

What am I without your directionless
abandonment.

Your not-ness.

The ways music appears and disappears in an
instant.

Maybe music has always been the essence of
leaving —
The antidote,
Timelessness.

Who am I without all the ways I fail you?
Who am I if I cannot bumble through the coals of
your fire?
Your crucibles?
Your tests?

Even if some days I'm only sure of one thing,
Electronic dance music is better than the gospel of
Jesus.

Even if we know things together I could never
know alone,
What if what I have after straining for so long is
not enough?

* * *

I guess we all deserved a greater love that day.
What ever day it was for you.

Is There Anything Infinite?

I'm so sorry,
I'm at the center of something.

I'm so sorry,
I just can't seem to hold it up.

It's only because I care so much,
That I think the thing to do is carry it,
Wondering,

Is there anything infinite?
Is there anything infinite?!
Is there anything infinite…?

When love feels lost?
When I am alone?

I'm so sorry,
I'm holding up a world begging me to put her

down.
She doesn't need saving,
But, I do.

I do.

I'm so sorry,
I'm both Goddesses now,
And no one knows how.

No one knows how.

Let Fear Be the First,
Let Love Be the Last

Sometimes I forget how to remember important
things.
And sometimes I just let them slip away,
Because I tell myself the seeds that are meant to
grow will grow in me,
And it's fruitless to grasp as I'm losing things.

Consciousness overflows with precious moments in
a life flowing frantically forward and forward, Ever
changing.
A life cool to the touch like the freshwater of a
stream,
One you can drink from.

So much floats away.

I tell myself again and again,
Let fear be the first thing you forget,
Let love be the last.

I have to tell myself it's ok to let some things slip

away,
Like dreams and details,
Certain words of advice,
Memories,
People even,.

Ways I felt when I was younger,
Ways I felt yesterday.
The things I've seen and how I saw them.

All the thoughts that slip into my spoon as I dip it
into soup cold from pondering long enough to
forget it was warm once.
Long enough to forget that I've sat here waiting
for a time I could eat a meal with someone I love.

This I try to forget the most…this aloneness.
Because it's so often the most painful thing that
travels from my head to my heart and back again,
over and over again.
Sometimes I can move and rearrange my body so
that it doesn't seem so bad,
The wound of it.

But, often I just have to forget that I feel that way,
That way I see all the things I think I lack.

This I think is ok to forget.

* * *

But, then there are things I dive deep to retrieve,
Because I wonder what my life means without it,
Without that dream,
Without those words spoke in the twilight,
Without that way you smiled at me from across
the table.

And I wonder what it all means without it.

And I wonder if by having it - keeping it,
Repeating it a hundred times so I couldn't possible
forget,
Writing it down quickly so the pen can still feel
the heart of it,
So the paper wants to remember, too —
If having it means anything at all.

What it means I truly do not know.
What it means perhaps is a promise.

A secret.

Something not even all the dead magicians and
poets can tell me.

Because even poetry can't hold such a thing as this
meaning of things.
Poets have words for the most sweet fruit,
The most bitter pains,

The most awesome magic,
But not this.

This way to say the why and what matters in the
very end.

So I wonder what I can forget,
And what I can let slip,
And what I must grasp.
But grasping is exhausting some days,
I let more go than maybe I should.
Because I am just hoping I can get on with the rest
-

The dishes and the art and the correspondences,
Lunches, walks and rest -
And I am always moving onward,
Forgetting how to remember it all,
Hoping I did not leave the most important thing
behind.

And I tell myself again and again,

Let fear be the first thing to forget,
Let love be the last.

Yellow Threads

Mother, Mother

I've read that the word, Mother,
However it is uttered,
Is at the root of all language.

That is why we say it when we die.

Mother, Mother
In the darkness we pray it,
Even if we knew the cruelest kind.

Mother, Mother
We seek her perfect,
In all of time,
Because we are all children,
Something we cannot deny.

Yet we are truly so close to forgetting the root,
Of creation.

Mother mother
Look what I found!

What is it, please?

Mother mother
Wait for me!

Show me,
What there is to eat.
What to fear.
Who to trust.

Mother, mother

Let us walk together.
Show me the way back home through the forest.

Mother, mother
Why do you weep?
Why are you hiding?

Why are we running?

Mother, mother

What have we done?
Can it be stopped?

Can we heal what has been broken?

Mother, mother

* * *

Wake up.

Mother, mother
Hold my hand.

Mother mother
Is my pain yours now?
Has yours always been mine, too?

Mother, mother
Help me find what I have lost.

Mother, mother
I have so many questions still.
Teach me how to love again.

Mother, mother
Help me let go into sleep.

Sing me that lullaby.
The one Grandma sang to you,
Sing it to me while I fall asleep.

Mother, mother
Who are we?
Why is the sky filled with our screams?

Mother.

***

Mother.

Mercy.

Please.

Universe of Leaving

When the questions first came,
A quizzical consciousness slipped in —
My young brain tripped up on invisible wire.

Just there in the way I started to ask,
Why did she leave?
Where has she gone?
What should become of something so great?
Something greater than what was?

Something to seek.
To clear a path,
No,
Force your way to.

My life —
Built on the questions that came.
Asked again and again.
Different ways but all the same.

* * *

A girl exhausted again,
Everything unanswered still.

Why do we leave?
What anger and pain it makes us eat.
Subsiding on just rage some days.

All the denied the humanity,
Of a lonely soul wandering through a universe of
leaving,
A universe of goodbyes and whys.

What Exiles I Have Known

What exiles I have known?

My God.

Out of the Earth of my mother's womb.
Then still, there is more —
Air, sound, pain, breath.

Ways and ways and ways we learn our un-
belonging —
Our division.
Ways and ways and ways of losing.

The great lesson of being separate.

My God.

This heart has never been un-broken.
Born to heal in the specter of Death.
Born to stumble in exile again and again.

One after the last.
The more precious the love,
The more violent the extraction.

Some lesson this is —
Trying to be made,
Despite all of the gathering up.

A reminder that knowing anything,
Is losing everything that we love.

And you,
In the fiery gate,
You're squinting mind,
On the other side,
You find out the truth.

Exile is a gift,
You are meant to become made,
Alongside it —
With it.

You see,
You will live and you will die like everything else.

That is the becoming itself.

Ten Thousand Times

Her body moved that way ten thousand times,
In her green dress.
Locking up the flower shop for the night.

I could see it happening again and again,
And all at once —
How time can occur like that in my mind
sometimes.

How I can see the son she lost,
And her joy in the smell of lavender on a Sunday.
The day she held him again.
And I can see the man she loved,
How he watched,
While she moved her body that way,
Again and again,
Until the end.

We are beautiful.
We are so beautiful.

* * *

The lives we keep alive.

The loves, like rain on the soil of it.
The sons we raise.
The lovers we lose to old age.
The things we do a thousand times,
On our way to our own graves.

For Josephine

The burnt Earth.
The bent path.
The Cardinal on the sill.

For the mothers, daughters, lovers and friends.
For Josephine.

Do you know what exhaustion feels like?
The modern kind?
The kind that is sick, angry and forgotten?
The kind filled to the brim with sorrow?

The kind that sees the steep price of a smile,
And smiles anyway.

The one voice trying to be a symphony,
Trying to be the soothing sound it needs.

She is trying to sing,
The stories she sees in the trees.

In each branch,

She is trying to sing,
The same song as the bird on her sill,
Smiling at her.

And I'm driving to the grocery store.
Wondering what is buried in all these suburban
yards?
Things to be forgotten?
Things never to be forgotten?
Things to be remembered only just enough?

And I am remembering Josephine.
The burnt Earth.

How the path is bent and bent.

I am remembering,
The things we bury,
And how exhausting it is to be forgotten.

Women Who Serve

Tinkering the airplane's gauges,
Years later,
Remembering the boys she knew,
Who died that day.

They always came to her to fix the broken things,
The cracked altitude readers.
The ones that she could see spinning —
Spinning all the way,

Down.

She remembers at the creek kissing him behind the
red barn,
And the black eye she gave him on the play
ground.

Peace.

She waits for peace when the lunch horn sounds.
And all the ladies scurry.

All the ladies are waiting for peace, too.

Peace.
In the kitchen that day.
He was so quiet when he slid his hands around her
waste,
While she made the coffee.

Peace.
She thought the sunlight was made out of
something eternal,
When he was warm and by her side.

Focus.
Forcing her eyes to tinker with the gauges.
All the boys knew she was the best,
At fixing broken things.

She could stop that spinning pin,
Mend the cracked shield,

The one in her mind though,
Kept spinning.

Spinning.

As she fixed the memory of a boy she might have
kissed by the creek.
Arms falling,

Dangling like disconnected wires,
Soon to be joined again in heaven.

White Threads

Gratitude is a Kaleidoscope

Gratitude is a telescope.
Gratitude is a satellite.
Gratitude is a kaleidoscope,
A microscope,
A mirror.

Gratitude is refusing to profit from love.

Gratitude is seeking no vengeance for loss.

No reconciliation for pain.
Just to turn a degree or two,
So you can see all the ways you are being held,
Right now.

Right now, you are being given grace.
Right now, the light awaits.
For your eyes to be the eyes that see it,
For your ears to be the ears that hear it.

Gratitude is grace.

* * *

Gratitude is peace in the storm of hate.

Gratitude is accepting death,
While you strive for more life,
And poetry,
And love,
And wisdom.

We take what we take.
We give only what we know we have to give,
What we see as abundant.

Wearing white on Sunday,
We pray.
Colors divided in the prism of light,
Colors, like people, find each other sometimes.

Gratitude is how we reunite.

Gratitude is a satellite
Gratitude is a telescope,
Microscope, Kaleidoscope
A mirror.

Gratitude is life.

Mary, My Grandmother

When I think of the golden necklace,
Laid on the skin of my Grandmother's chest —
A tiny shrine to Mother Mary,
I think of how little there is left.
And yet, so much more that is precious.

I think of worship,
And a golden thread of hope.
And the love that feels hidden —
In the early days of separation.
When I am living without the breath,
The heart space,
Where my Grandmother,
And a golden Mary prayed.

It reminds me that love might be like looking into
the past,
And knowing none of it belongs to you.

And into the future, too.

That you must let it all go.

And then,
Maybe,
Some miracle will make you a child of it.

Like a golden hope.
Like an altar of breath,
And Mary's love on your Grandmother's chest.

Make It Rain

Some days,
I live in the shadow of things much grander than
me.

But whether I am someone or no-one,
I go into the world as medicine,
While most go as thieves.

If I am not blessed or believed by society,
I am blessed each morning by the Sun.
By the wind,
By the plants and the flowers,
By the uncomplicated sound of bird song.

Do I mourn my exile? Yes.
But, I am not willing to sit and cry by the water —
Any longer.

She says to me again,
"Make it rain."

* * *

Make it rain.
And I think, directionless,
In a kind of panic —
What is the rain and how do I make it come?
Is the rain of my heart or is of my head?

Is it a story not told yet?
A poem not sung?

"I'll sing it!" I say.
But, I don't know the song.

I just wander through my life and try to be what I
am.

The rain,
The rain.

Where the Saints Loved?

You asked me once,
Where the saints loved?

The way they brooded and sang,
The chronic pain of the new way?

Do you not remember the warnings,
My friend?

Don't covet the dreamers dreams,
The saint's songs.
They sing in rivers of fire,
And cross them to carry sweet things,
To your more isolate shore.

Yes, did you know,
Your shore is the most remote of them all?

You asked,
Were the saints loved?

The way you wished they were?
The way you hoped they'd be?
The way you sometimes are?

No, no, my friend.
Don't you remember the warnings?

Don't covet the dreamer's dream.
Don't covet the poet's devotion.
Or the saint's song.

Don't covet the lands they travel in.
There is no treasure there for you,
If you are not prepared for each and every death
you'll encounter there.

Are you ready to be ugly and utterly alone?
No, this has never been a well everyone should
drink from.

No, do you not remember the warnings?

Don't covet the dreamers dream.
Don't covet the poet's devotion.
Or the saint's song.

Stay safe in your listening for the way home.

Stay safe in all the ways they might be wrong.

I Am My Own Saint Now

I am my own saint now.
Let the other saints be released.

I am alone and unmastered.

Un-fascinated by fame.

Enamored by breath,
And all the ways I might love.

The purest of the summer songs —
The purest to be.

The almost heart.

I am my own saint now.

To Find a Song

When we finally find our song,
The one that called to us from deep within,
When we were young,
The song that fell from the stars into our lungs.
The song that felt lost from that very moment on.

When we finally find its rhythm and its rhyme,
The way it beats,
Just the same as our own heart does.
The way its melody and its frequency,
Is the why of how we see what we see.

When we find the notes,
And the tone,
A sacred text is encrypted there —
Translate it.
And hold the puzzle and all the pieces,
In your hands.

Look back on when it first called to you,

It was so, so, long ago, I know.
I was so, so, young, too.

See the bravery in each and every step we took,
In a world bent on distortion,
Bent on extracting us from that path back.
From the slow opening of our ears to hear,
The song that we were longing for,
In each and every step we took.

In a world that tore up and scattered the map.
All the clues long lost in eons of forgetting.
In the empty fields and floods of silence.
We searched and searched and searched for that
sound.
We followed the sent of the of it loss in our bellies,
Our mouths sputtering poetry,
Like sirens, like lighthouses to reunite something
long lost.

And sometimes, we were so close we could taste it.
But, we might have became accustom to losing it,
And loving our lostness.

The universe is tolerant,
And the song would never truly abandon us,
Even if we mistook her for a joke.

* * *

And after so much trouble,
So much traveling,
So much seeking,
We wake up to the sound of our song in the
morning wind,
In the feeling of the sun on our skin.

And when that sound hits the water of our bodies
again,
It heals us.
In this strange way some part of us wonders,

Who was this song really for?

And then,
We start to remember how to make it into an
offering.

Although our voices are shy and quivering,
We learn the drum.
We play it like a hummingbird at first
But then we learn to let the mother in us,

Slow it down.

© Karin Jervert 2024